1

Bunny Miner

Desert Shadow Publishing
1561 S. Karen Dr.
Chandler, AZ 85286
www.bunnyminer.com
Publisher's Note: This is a work of fiction. Names, characters, places, and incidents are a product of the author's imagination. Locales and public names are sometimes used for atmospheric purposes. Any resemblance to actual people, living or dead, or to businesses, companies, events, institutions, or locales is completely coincidental.
Book design © 2015, Desert Shadow Publishing
ISBN 978-1503086630
Printed in the United States of America

And So It Begins...

INTRODUCTION

If you have been writing for any length of time, you've probably heard of NaNoWriMo. If you have participated in it, you know what a crazy ride it is! If you are new to NaNoWriMo, here's the skinny:

NaNoWriMo stands for National Novel Writing Month. This high intensity writing challenge has taken place every November since 1999 and grew to over 450,000 participants in 2013. Since their inception, over two hundred and fifty traditionally published novels have come into existence because of this challenge. Some of the greats include Gruen's *Water for Elephants*, Morgenstern's *The Night Circus*, Howey's *Wool*, Rowell's *Fangirl*, Hough's *The Darwin Elevator*, and Meyer's *Cinder*.

Each November aspiring authors, educators and students embark on the challenge to write 50,000 words from November 1st to November 30th. The rules are pretty simple, don't start the actual writing part of your novel until November 1st (you can have outlines, plot notes, character descriptions, etc.) and keep cranking until you hit 50,000. The crew over at theNaNoWriMo website work hard to keep you motivated and educated. The other participants are around the forums to help out as well.

This book is a selection of one page story beginnings to help get your creative juices flowing. The idea is that it will help you complete your own novel in a month, be it January or November. If the muse strikes, don't wait! Start writing now, or get all your background work done between the time you pick up this book and the next NaNoWriMo. Then hit the ground running.

WRITING TIPS

If you're planning this big of an undertaking (writing a novel in 30 days), you have to get organized. Here are some tips that I've learned through trial and error and some I've picked up from talking to other writers:

Organization

Whether you're an outliner or a fly by the seat of your pants kind of writer (pantser for short!), organization is the key to completing a challenge like this. In my opinion everyone is an outliner, just some writers do it externally (the outliner bunch) and some writers do it internally (the pantser crowd). If you are planning on writing your novel 'organically' and just letting the muse take you where it wants to lead, you'll be too scattered to make sufficient progress to complete a thirty-day-novel-writing challenge. Can a novel be written this way? Of course! Your plot just meanders around for a while and the writing requires more edits and re-writes. That being said, your next step is to sit down and organize your time.

Time Management

Life happens. None of us (I hope!) lives in a vacuum. We have jobs, we have kids, we have other responsibilities. We are unable to write twenty-four hours a day/seven days a week. So figure out realistically how much time you can devote to writing each day. Yes, in order to complete this feat you have to write every day, whether the muse shows up or not.

Be Consistent

Write EVERY DAY! Whether you get up earlier each day for the next thirty days or go to bed later, you have to find a way to steal time from your normal routine to write. If you think you're going to write in your spare snippets of time, you're wrong. Something will always come up to challenge you for that time slot, and in most cases, it will win. You need to make an appointment with yourself and schedule a time to write every day. Then you have to protect that time. Nothing else can take precedence (well, if the house is burning or the kids are spurting blood, I guess you can put off your writing...). It doesn't have to be the same time every day but it does need to be scheduled. How long that time period is really depends on you. How many words do you write in an hour? In a half hour? Don't worry about each word being the best word possible, just get the story idea out and on paper. You won't be completing a publishable novel in this time frame, you'll be getting a first draft done. If you can't think of the perfect word to describe your heroine's hair as *it blows in the shock wave created by an explosion* (please avoid overusing adjectives as the easy way out!), just put an xxx or a *** and move on. You can fill in the blanks later when you re-write, revise and edit. Again, this time is to just get the story on paper. You'll be perfecting it later.

Word Count Vs. Time Spent

I can't tell you how much time or how many words you should to write each day. That will depend on you. Once you figure out how much time you can carve out in your schedule, work backwards to figure out if that time frame is realistic for getting your novel written. Say, for example, you figured you could devote thirty minutes a day to this challenge, you'd have to write 1666 words in that time. It is possible but not realistic. You'd have to type fifty-five words per minute, non-stop for thirty minutes. Remember that's organic writing, not copying from some other text. Again, it is possible, but you'd be better off figuring out how to get more writing time each day. For me a comfortable pace is be closer to two hours a day. That's roughly two pages an hour or four pages a day based on three to five hundred words per page. If you're on a roll and you have the time, for heaven's sake, don't stop writing! However, be careful not to let this take over your life. Your other obligations still need to be met. If you do have the time, though, keep going until you have to stop but most people can squeeze two hours out of their day. Remember this isn't a forever thing (unless you can do it forever, in which case, you'll be a mighty prolific writer!), it's just thirty days. If this is truly important to you, you can make the sacrifice of your favorite show or whatever you have to give up for thirty days. One last thought on the time you invest——though it's best to write all in one sitting, if you need to break up your writing time, that's okay! The important thing is to make a goal and stick to it. 'Get 'er done!' as Larry the Cable Guy would tell you.

Create a Writing Space

The next tip for getting organized is to find a place to write. Some people like to write to music, some like it quiet. My personal preference is to be left alone with just me and my thoughts and ideas. But as I have four very active kids, that's a pipe dream! As I write, my son is blasting 80's music and singing at the top of his rather out of tune lungs and my daughter keeps coming in to show me the blackmail video she has shot of him. Now mind you, I've been writing for years (I started when I only had two very young ones) and no matter how often I ask my kids to leave me alone when I write at home, there's always something they deem as life or death that needs my attention RIGHT NOW. For me, my most productive writing time is spent away from home. It's not always possible for everyone to do that, but you do need to establish your own writing space. Make it something that fits your personality. Not everyone has the luxury of having a spare room to write in, but even if it's only a card table with a folding chair in the corner of your bedroom or kitchen, set it up with things that will inspire you to write. Tape pictures on the wall, get your favorite writing instrument if you write by hand, and make that your go-to space when you have your scheduled writing time. You want to do this for a couple of reasons. One reason is because your mind will associate this space with writing, not watching TV or doing the dishes or whatever you would do in other spaces in your house. Another reason is because you need to respect yourself and your writing craft enough to make this place special and distinct. Make it your own.

Suggested Reference Materials

So, now you know how much time you have, you've broken it down to a words-per-day goal and you've found a place to write. Now you're ready to start *thinking* about the writing process. Since this isn't a how-to-write book, I'd like to share a couple of books that I have found helpful in my own writing career. Over the years I've read many books about how to write a novel. One of my favorite books about the writing process is *Save the Cat* by Blake Snyder. Even though this is a book written primarily for screen writers, the material contained in it applies to all types of writing. Snyder shows writers how to break down the writing process into a series of beats. This is great information for outliner and pantser alike. Another way I've seen the breakdown of a novel described is in acts. One book that does this is *Structuring Your Novel: Essential Keys for Writing an Outstanding Story by K. M. Weiland*. Weiland breaks down the novel into three acts then breaks each act down even further. Weiland teaches you about plot points, inciting events, climaxes, and resolutions. This is definitely a book that should be in your writing library.

Bunny Miner

The Gold in *This* Book

This book is all about helping you come up with an initial idea to write about. It has been designed to give you twelve months of one page story beginnings to get your creative juices flowing. You may end up keeping some of the starter or go in a completely different direction. What you come up with based on these story beginnings will be completely unique to you. I've discovered that when a room of people are given a story starter, no two are alike. So find an idea and run with it. The sky's the limit!

Let Your Idea Grow

After picking your first story starter, resist the urge to start writing immediately. Let the idea brew for a bit in your mind. If you're an outliner, sit down in a day or so and organize the thoughts that have developed. If you're a pantser, wait that same day or two to let the pot simmer then sit down and start writing. A lot happens in your subconscious that will really help you in the writing process, so make sure to allow time for your subconscious to go to work.

Limit Distractions

One last tip that I recently learned. I used to write by hand because I really enjoyed the feel of pen on paper, but over the last few years I've switched to keyboard composing. I think both methods work well so pick whichever you're comfortable with. However, if you're a keyboard composer, TURN OFF YOUR SPELL CHECK, log out of the internet and dim your

6

background screen. I never thought it was a big deal to write with the spell check on until I took the *30 Day Kindle Challenge* by Kristen Eckstein. She made this suggestion to those of us in taking the course, and I thought it was just a formality until I sat down to write. Those blasted colored lines made me go back and change things instead of just letting my ideas flow. I found I write much more quickly when it is off. Now that I've mentioned it, they'll probably start driving you crazy, too. So while you are writing your first draft, turn off the spell check and don't turn it back on until you're ready to edit. As for the internet, everyone knows what a time-suck it can be. Just try to go look up only one thing on Pinterest!

Scrivner is a writing program that you can purchase that can assist in many aspects of your writing. Limiting distractions is one of them. Scrivner will do all the afore mentioned items for you but there's a pretty steep learning curve so don't try to learn Scrivner and write a novel at the same time!

Now it's time to turn the page, take a look at some stories I've started for you, and pick the one which resonates with you the most!

Happy writing!

Note from the Author: As this is a copyrighted piece of work, these story starters are intended as just a jumping off point for your own writing. Copying my starter word for word is plagiarism. Please keep that in mind if you plan to publish the work you develop based on the story starter. If you have any questions about whether or not there would be a copyright issue, please feel free to contact me.

AND SO IT BEGINS...

JANUARY

So this is what death feels like. Hmm, not really what I was expecting. Honestly, though, as
a twelve year old I mostly spend my time thinking about baseball, school and girls. Not
necessarily in that order.

What happens now? Do I just wait? Isn't there supposed to be a light or something? Currently, black seems to be the only color making an appearance.

"James Patrick Sullivan?" said the man with a clipboard who just came out of a door that appeared out of nowhere.

"That's me," I said. I raised my arm so he could see where I was sitting.

Hey! When did my body get here? Wait! You get a body in heaven? Is this heaven?

I shivered, realizing my head was attached again and tried not to remember how I...well...how it...well, how I ended up here.

"Follow me, please."

With that he walked back through the door. The door closed with a whisper of sound behind him. Luckily I could still see the door.

Do I really want to follow him? Anything could be behind that door. It could be the entrance to heaven but since how I got here wasn't exactly legal, it could just as easily be the way to hell.

I looked around the waiting room that materialized about the same time as Clipboard Guy, the door, and my body. I noticed there was a soft, white glow around everything. It looked like a shimmering mist. The bench I was sitting on was a white wood-like material and connected to the white walls about three quarters the way around the entire white room. I looked down at my lap and realized I even have on white pants. Everything here is white except the kids. Staring around the room, I realize that everyone looks about my same age. All of us have the same white clothes on, though we seem to cover every ethnicity on the planet.

Is this some sort of uniform? Why would we need a uniform in heaven?

11

I'm not sure how long I gawked at the room and its inhabitants but I jumped when the door opened and Clipboard called my name again. I clamped my jaw shut and decided this time I should probably follow him. Maybe this was my only way into heaven.

"Could you call me Jake?"

"As you wish, Jake."

I follow Clipboard though the door. This definitely is *not* heaven.

FEBRUARY

Ariel turned the stone over and over in her hand. Could this be the one? The size was right. Just about as big as her palm. Surely it would grow with her. The color was right. If you could really call it a color...it was more like a rainbow hue that twisted and changed along with her mood. Other stones had been able to mimic the seer stone. She'd been fooled before, and it had cost her people dearly. The weight was definitely right. This was the first time she'd felt one so light.

It seemed the time of the prophecy was at hand. Was she ready?

"What have you got there, M'lady?"

Ariel jumped as she put the rock beneath her robe not wanting anyone to see.

"Nothing, Jasper. Just looking for rocks to skip on the water."

Ariel put on her innocent face and continued to search the shore for rocks. Occasionally she'd pick up a stone and plunk it into the lake. It was always a good idea to keep her precision throwing-skills hidden. She also took care to keep her other skills hidden as well. Ariel knew the danger of revealing her secret. The secret that cost her parents their lives.

"Jasper, isn't this a pretty rock?" She said as she held out an ordinary-looking stone. "I must keep it for my collection. Here, carry it for me."

It wouldn't do to have anyone who might be lurking about to know that she had more than a ladyship/guardian relationship with Jasper. And he played his part equally well.

"As you wish, M'lady." Jasper put the rock in the basket along with the other stones Ariel had collected that day. Jasper knew his young charge was looking for something. He had prepared her well for her role in the coming battles, but she never trusted him completely. Ariel still kept many things to herself.

For the past four years Jasper trained Ariel to fight, to think, to rule. All to fulfill the promise he made to her late father. He tried hard to keep his emotions in check, but

And So It Begins...

Jasper's shoulders slumped as he thought of the king. So young, merely in his twenties. So full of promise, yet cut short of fulfilling it. Luckily, he was able to pass his mission on to his daughter. Only eight at the time. It was a miracle she understood the importance of it. Yet, Ariel had always seemed an old soul. Somber and willing to do whatever was asked of her. Able to keep a secret. She had not even told Jasper what she knew of her mission. After all, her father had told her to tell no one.

Jasper knew the secret, though. He kept his knowledge of it from Ariel just as she kept her knowledge a secret from him. The time would come when he would reveal to her all that he knew but not until she fulfilled her part of the mission. That she would have to do thinking she was completely alone. Thinking she was on her own would keep her safe. It was the only way her powers would fully materialize.

MARCH

Ten seconds to go and Maggie had the ball. Jason slipped out his foot, tripping her to stop her forward progress to the basket.

"What did you do that for?" she said as she picked herself up from the floor and started toward him, fists clenched at her sides. This wasn't the first time Jason took Maggie out of a game. She wasn't going to let him get away with it.

Warning whistles blew from all sides of the court as Maggie took a swing at Jason. Within seconds the team was off the bench pulling them apart. Again.

"You can't foul your own teammate!" the ref yelled. "Both of you, out! Go cool off in the locker rooms."

"Stupid girl," Jason muttered under his breath as he pushed past her. Maggie stepped back to keep her balance.

Following Jason towards the locker room, Maggie paused in the doorway and bent down pretending to tie her shoe as the last seconds ticked by on the clock. At the final buzzer the score was 87-88, the other team.

Maggie's ears burned as she thought of Jason tripping her. *What the crap was his problem?* Maggie knew some of the guys weren't exactly thrilled with having a girl on the school team, but Maggie knew she was good. She knew she carried her weight.

After showering and getting dressed in girl-like clothing, Maggie headed out of the locker room to meet her friends in the parking lot. Win or lose, pizza was always in order after a game.

"What took you so long, girl? We're starving out here!"

Maggie smiled as she ran to catch up with her friends. At least with them she didn't have something to prove. Plus, she knew they had her back.

"What's up with Anderson? He cost us the game," said Sarah, Maggie's best friend.

"I have no idea, but it's getting old. The other guys have gotten over the whole 'we don't want a girl on our team' thing, but Jason just won't let it go. It's not like I bring the team down. I scored 40 of our 87 points. That's almost half of the total score. I don't want to talk about basketball. Tell me what happened with you and Marty!"

The two girls giggled as they headed for Sarah's brother's car. Being fifteen meant you had to rely on someone else to drive, but Maggie didn't mind. Sarah's brother was kind of cute. Since he just got his license, he was happy to drive them anywhere. Especially if it involved food.

"Hey, Gregg. Thanks for the ride."

"Pish—are you kidding? Sarah would have made something up to our parents, and I wouldn't have gotten the car at all if I didn't drive you guys. Jump in. I'm hungry and you're buying!"

Pulling up to the pizza place, Maggie shuddered as she saw Jason walking into the restaurant.

APRIL

Just keep moving forward. Keep your eyes down. Navia thought of her mother's words. They echoed over and over in her mind.

"You! Jew! Step out of the line." The venom in the guard's voice was evident, and Navia shuddered as she dared to look up.

The guard was looking at someone else. Navia moved on, tension almost dissolving from her weary body. Almost, but not quite. Closer to the train she inched. She pulled the sweater she wore to cover her star tighter around her shoulders. She couldn't get caught. She knew it would mean death. Not only to her but to the Van Housen family who were taking her with them to

England. Their departure had been so hasty that Navia didn't even have time to change out of her Ghetto clothes. They simply tried to cover them.

Thinking of her mother tore at her heart. Would she ever see her again? And Papa. Navia didn't even get to say goodbye to him. Maybe they would stay safe. Maybe they would stay hidden. But the Nazis raided the Ghetto more every day. There was talk of them even sealing it off. Would her parents get out before then? Navia knew that they had sent her with the Van Housens because they were afraid the Nazis were closing the Ghetto soon. *Please let them meet me in England,* Navia prayed, not for the first time since she left.

After what seemed like hours, they were safely aboard the train. The Van Housens had money so they were able to secure a private car. Once they closed and locked the doors, and pulled the curtains, they sat down across from Navia.

"Navia, I know this is scary," Mrs. Van Housen said in a hushed voice, "but we've done this before. Many times. What we need you to do is memorize your new identity. You're now Mary Hughes. We are your aunt and uncle and are taking you to visit your grandparents in England. You are an American. We will help you with your accent."

American? Navia had never even seen an American. How was she going to act like one? Plus, didn't the Germans hate the Americans?

"Can I go to the bathroom before we begin?" Navia slipped out of the seat into their private bathroom. The tears started to fall almost as soon as she closed the door.

Please God, please, let my family be safe. Navia felt guilty for leaving them. She knew leaving Germany was dangerous, but she felt as if her family was in even more danger staying. How could people be so cruel? Just because of the God she chose to worship? None of it made sense to Navia, but she knew she had to be strong. Her parents had risked a lot to send her with the Van Housens. She had to be brave and find a way to help them once she was out of Germany.

"Are you okay in there?" Mrs. Van Housen lightly tapped on the door. "Don't be afraid. I promise we'll make this as easy as possible for you. Please come out. We don't have very long."

Navia knew she was right. She wiped away her tears, splashed some cold water on her face, and squaring her shoulders, opened the door.

MAY

The salt in the air soothed Brandon's agitation. As he paddled his board out, the tension began to release from his muscles, his shoulders relaxing. The ocean spray clung to his hair as he caught another wave. Here, he was safe.

As he cutback over the wave in one smooth, fluid move, his mind wandered back to his day at school. Brandon hated English. Everything about it screamed he was dumb. The harder he tried the worse it seemed to get. He concentrated on the words in the book but they never stayed still. Today Mrs. Dustin asked him to read out loud again. Did she really need to humiliate him like that every week?

"B-b-brandon. C-c-come on, r-e, r-e, read to us," mocked Michael from behind him. Never loud enough for her to hear but always enough to make reading even worse for Brandon. He stuttered, he lost his place, he turned red. This brought even more jeers from behind. Brandon couldn't get to the beach quick enough today.

As he reached the shore this time, he swore and slammed his board onto the sand. Even surfing wasn't going to turn his mind off. Maybe it was time to talk to someone about things. His mom kept trying to get him to go to a shrink. What would they do though? Tell him to try harder? To ignore Michael? He had been doing that since they arrived on the Big Island. It wasn't working!

Brandon knew he wasn't dumb, but it still bothered him that other people did. Back in California, the kids he had grown up with had gotten used to Brandon's stuttering and the time it took him to get through even the simplest passages. They actually made him feel like he accomplished something big when he got through a reading assignment. Here, the islanders seemed ignorant and mean.

Brandon's mom told him how much he'd love it here. He could go to school half a day then hit the beach to practice every day. He didn't have to drive an hour to get to the ocean like he did back home. She painted a picture of perfection, the childhood home she remembered as if it had been a dream. Maybe it had been her dream, but it was turning out to be Brandon's nightmare.

"Hey, brah. Nobody should look that glum on a perfect wave day like today. Not even a houlee, like you." It was Kahakili, one of the surfer friends Brandon made on his first day here.

"When I see you eat it, I think I'll be able to muster a smile," Brandon tossed back.

"You're on, brah. Let's hit the line up and let Kanaloa claim you as his son."

The remaining tension was erased from Brandon's mind and heart as they hit the waves together. Maybe his mom had been right after all. Maybe Hawaii was the paradise for which they had been searching. At least this far from L.A. his dad's fists couldn't reach either of them. He just had to remember to not reveal anything from their past.

JUNE

Alice stared at the letter in her hand. A small tremor ran down her arm and shook the envelope. She licked her lower lip and swallowed over the lump in her throat. Was this really it? She wasn't sure what she wanted it to say. If it had the name she was searching for, it would change her life forever. *If the name was there, what would she do with it?*

Well really, how much more would it change her life? Everything she thought she knew changed three months ago when she needed that blood transfusion, and she discovered neither of her parents were a match, meaning only one thing. They weren't her real parents. After a lot of denial and a lot of tears, her mother finally confessed the horrible truth. They had lied to her her entire life. She wasn't their daughter. She wasn't Alice Swapp. She was

25

nobody. She had no past, no future, until she answered the question burning in her mind. Who was she really, and why didn't her real parents want her? Who were they, and, as a result, who was she?

Taking a deep breath and blowing it out through clenched teeth, she ripped off the end of the envelope and shook out the paper inside. The paper that was about to change her life.

"What's wrong, Alice? You look like you've lost your puppy or something?" The woman she had called mom for the past 16 years tried to get her to open up with a shaky smile. Alice hadn't talked to her since she had told her the truth. Even though Evelyn tried everyday, Alice refused to let her in. Refused to forgive her.

I should have done this in my room, thought Alice as she looked around the small entryway of the place she had called home. The tile was cracked in the corner by the door where she remembered sitting with a hammer when she was four thinking if she could get below the tile slab she might uncover a treasure. Evelyn hadn't yelled at her. Instead she sent her into the backyard with a small shovel and bucket, suggesting a treasure might be buried out there and not in the house. The small antique table where the mail was put everyday stood between her and Evelyn, but the distance between them was much greater. Alice almost showed her the letter. Almost let Evelyn put her arms around her like she had done a thousand times before. She almost let her be the mom she had always been. Almost, but not quite.

Alice turned around and headed up the stairs to her room. Away from Evelyn, away from the life she knew. She closed the door with just barely enough force for it to catch, closed out her old life and sat on her bed to accept her new life. The life she should have had.

Stop being a scaredy cat. Open it. And with that thought she unfolded the letter that would change her life forever. A letter that revealed more than she ever imagined.

JULY

True love's kiss? True love's KISS? They couldn't be serious! Florian didn't even like girls and the thought of kissing one just about made him throw up. Add to that the fact that she was technically dead—no way!

True, the prophecy had been quoted since the beginning of time, but no way was it going to be him. He had no idea why his parents made him listen to this every single year. His father didn't have to kiss a dead girl. His grandfather didn't have to kiss a dead girl. In fact, no Valiant had EVER had to kiss a dead girl, and the tradition certainly wasn't going to start with him. Man, what a way to spend your birthday.

Florian tuned out the lecture soon after he heard the words 'glass coffin'. His mind wandered to a chorus of blah, blah, blah, blah, blah. Instead, he was mentally off fighting dragons and sharpening swords.

"Did you hear what I said, Your Highness?" squawked Master Preston, his new tutor.

"Um, not really," he said with a shrug.

"Well unless you start to pay attention to your studies, you'll never be fit to run a kingdom."

"You're talking about kissing dead girls. What does that have to do with running a kingdom?"

"Proper steps must be taken to ensure your princess is not faking or in some way poisoned."

"I thought the whole story was about her being poisoned. I've been listening to it since I was a baby."

"Not being poisoned herself! In some way able to poison *you*. Many people would like to see you fail in your attempt to rouse your true love."

"Wait! Nobody ever said anything about ME being poisoned. Definitely not going to kiss a stiff if I'm likely to get poisoned. Can't we just hire someone to do the kissing? Besides, what is the likelihood of it being me? No one in our bloodline has ever had to find their dead true love. Chances aren't likely it'll start with me."

"That's where you're wrong, sir. With each passing generation that doesn't have to kiss the enchanted princess, the likelihood of the following generation being the one who will have to do the deed increases."

Was he serious? His chances were greater? There was no way Florian was kissing a dead chick. Uh-uh, no way. He had to get out of here.

As soon as instruction ended for the day, Florian bolted to his room and threw open the closet doors. Surely there was something in here that he could use as a sack. Being a prince had its perks but when it came to finding things you never had to touch, it made stealth rather difficult. *Come on, come on, where was a knapsack?* After a fruitless search, Florian grabbed his pillow and shook it from its case. His mother would be angry at him for ruining the matching set, but there was no way he was going to spend another day here if his destiny was to kiss a dead girl who was going to poison him. Yep, he was moving on.

AUGUST

Excitement made Jeremy jittery as he realized he was at THE Rossfield Academy. Even though his lucky ticket in came from the lottery, at least he was here! Most of the kids chosen from Jeremy's class got here on merit alone, but try as he might, his grades were never good enough.

"Students, you are here because you deserve to be here. Know that and no longer worry about it. Your neighbor is here because he or she deserves it. There will be no discussion of this in the future. This will not cause any rifts in your groups." The man's voice was gruff and powerful. This was not someone Jeremy wanted to mess with.

31

If they're bringing up why people are here already, it's bound to be a big deal. Great. Several of his classmates looked his way. He was an outcast, on the first day.

"You will find that what you learn here will be nothing like your regular school studies. You can forget what you think you know about education and be prepared to have your mind expanded beyond what you ever thought possible."

This was so cool. Ever since he was young, Jeremy heard stories about the elite Rossfield Academy for the Gifted. His father went there, his grandfather went there, and his great grandfather helped found it, but he never thought he'd have a chance to go. Molly was the brain in the family, not him, and since only one child could attend from a family, Jeremy never thought it would be him. Until the accident.

"In the packet you received upon arrival, you will find a color-coded badge. You will wear this badge at all times while on campus. You will leave them here when you go home on visiting weekends but, other than that, they must be with you at all times. You may now open your packet and take them out."

They were instructed to not open the packet until the headmaster told them to do so. Jeremy couldn't wait to see what was inside. With an air of reverence, Jeremy slipped his finger beneath the lip of the envelope and slid it carefully across the edge so as not to rip it any more than necessary. Nerves made his hands shake even though he was excited to see what they had given the new students.

With great care, Jeremy shook the contents of the envelope out onto the desk he was sitting at. The contents included the colored badge the headmaster spoke of, an odd looking key, a thumb drive, and a gun.

With his heart rate accelerating and sweat beginning to form on his upper lip, Jeremy looked around the room and saw that everyone else had received the same items in their packages. Nothing was ever mentioned about guns when his father spoke of Rossfield. What could possibly be going on here?

"The items you see before you will either save your life or take your life, so listen carefully to the instructions you receive over the next few weeks. Welcome to The Trial."

SEPTEMBER

September 1st, start of 8th grade

Dear Diary,

Today is the first day of the end of life as I have known it. My brother, the loser, has started junior high with me and I will never be able to show my face at school again. Being homeschooled can't possibly be as bad as having Lucian walking the same halls as I, eating in the same cafeteria that I have called my own for the last two years, and ruining the reputation that I have meticulously honed in everything I have said and worn. This truly is a travesty of justice that I simply do not know how to fix.

Goodbye cruel world!

Abby

September 2nd, the day my mother ruined my life

Dear Diary,

I simply do not understand it. I presented all the horrifying facts to my mother and she refused to call the school and withdraw me. She actually made me walk to school with Lucian! In public. Even though I tried to stay 20 paces ahead of him, he would do everything in his chubby power to keep up. Why does the universe hate me so? Why have I, of all people, been hindered by such an obtuse boy for a sibling? There is no justice in this life.

I go now to sob into my pillow. Goodnight!

Abby the Tortured

September 15th, Alas it has not improved

Dear Diary,

You are now my only true friend! I can't speak to any of my so-called friends at school. They find Lucian charming. Can you believe it? Lucian? Charming? Surely these past years with me have opened their eyes to the finer things in life. How could they let me down like this? I shan't be able to sleep this night for fear of the horrible dreams that await me. Yet, I must so that I do not look the tortured maiden I am in the morning. I will carry this burden alone. No one shall know of my troubles. I shall not let them see me in any light other than that of confidence and poise. I shall endure.

Be proud of me, dear diary, I will not be defeated.

Abby the Brave

OCTOBER

Bastian scurried across the field, his heart racing and his feet moving faster than he ever thought possible. He had to get the packet to Anastatia before she called for a war.

Overhead, a shadow passed him. He didn't take time to look up, knowing it would slow his progress. It was a move he would regret.

Without so much as a swoosh sound in the air, the hawk dropped down to the field and plucked Bastian up mid-stride. Bastian was too shocked to be scared and clutched the package close to his chest. He had to find a way to Anastatia! Too much was at stake. Without thinking it through, Bastian pulled his tiny sword from its scabbard and stabbed the hawk in the soft tuft over its chest. The hawk let out an ear-piercing screech, dropped Bastian, and soared away from the source of its pain. Meanwhile, Bastian began his plummet toward the earth as he sheathed his sword. Twisting and turning, head over heel, Bastian fell down, down, down. The wind whipped around him and between his body and the package. Bastian held it tighter then scrambled to keep his hold as the wind tore at it. After a terrifying few seconds, Bastian lost his hold on the package for a split second before regaining it again above his head. To his astonishment, and great luck, the package acted as a parachute and slowed his fall. Gently, on the current of the breeze, Bastian floated to the ground, across the field, and landed at the entrance to the tunnel that led to Anastatia's lair.

Bastian's nose twitched as he looked around to make sure nobody was watching. With care, he moved back the fake branches and squeezed inside the hole that led to the tunnels. The tunnel was usually guarded by badgers or ferrets. Bastian wondered how soon he would encounter them. Once again, Bastian unsheathed his sword. Waiting a moment for his eyes to adjust to the pitch dark, Bastian cautiously proceeded down the path. At the first turn, Bastian poked his head around the corner with the practiced speed of a warrior to search for trouble. The tunnel was empty.

Bastian's heartbeat slowed and his heightened senses relaxed. It was then that Bastian realized his sides hurt. Within seconds the hurt turned into a searing pain. He reached down to gingerly feel his side and pulled his hand away, sticky and wet. It was blood. His breaths turned to short pants and the corners of his vision turned black. Was this how it ended? Was he going to die with his destination so close?

Ripping a strip of cloth from his shirt, he tied it tightly around his mid-section. If he could just stem the flow of blood for a few more minutes, he could reach Anastatia. He could deliver the packet. He could save his world. He tore away another strip and shored up the bandages. Now, crawling more than running, Bastian continued down the tunnel. Soon he could see a light at the end and concentrated on it. Trying to not feel the pain, he put one foot in front of the other and focused on getting to the light. *One step, two, just keep going.* At last, when he thought he could go no further, he reached an illuminated door. What awaited him there, though, was not what he expected.

"It's you," he said with his final breath and collapsed in a heap on the damp, dank ground.

NOVEMBER

NaNoWriMo Time!

The sirens blared and the emergency lighting system kicked into gear. This was it, the end of the world. Adam had been taught this would happen in his lifetime but never really believed it. What twelve-year-old kid would? Everyone lives past twelve years old.

Knowing what he had to do, Adam grabbed the pre-packed bag of emergency goods and headed to the tunnels that lead to the shelter. It wouldn't guarantee survival but it was the best hope they had. The only hope they had. No adults followed them. They had been forbidden to follow. All around him, Adam witnessed tearful goodbyes and wishes of luck. Fools. They were wasting precious time.

Adam ran down the twists and turns that would lead him to the underbelly of the Earth. Presumably far enough enclosed in dirt and rock to be able to withstand the crashing of the space debris that had been threatening to fall to earth his whole life. When the lights of what appeared to be shooting stars filled the night, Adam knew that the time had come. He was prepared. Well, physically anyway. His heart raced as he dodged around the slower moving kids. He had to get as deep as possible as soon as possible. It was his only hope.

"Hey, watch where you're going! The world's not going to end without you, you can slow down." The snide comment caused Adam to pause. He turned around to see the owner of the voice and found himself face to face with the most interesting girl he had ever encountered. Her hair was shorn completely off one side of her head, and the opposite side was cut in all different angles and dyed every color of the rainbow. In her eyebrows, nose, and lip she sported small hoop-type rings. The thing that amazed him most, though, was the intricate patchwork of a tattoo that peeked out beneath her fringed hair. It glowed! Adam had never seen anything like it.

"Your face..." he began.

"What about it? Yours isn't much to look at either, prep."

Adam knew she was referring to his boarding school uniform and manicured hair, but the observation seemed to encompass all of him, not just his appearance, and he was offended.

"Look, if we want to have any hope of surviving this we have to get down to the unfinished parts of the tunnels. There's not enough depth here." Adam wasn't sure why he was concerned about helping this girl, but he was drawn to her for some unknown reason.

He grabbed her hand and started to pull her with him as he ran. Surprisingly, she followed him without any hesitation, matching him stride for stride. They pushed past the crowd that grew less and less dense the further they descended toward the tunnels. They only stopped for a moment when they reached the tunnels—the large, opened structure that housed cots and supplies and so many kids the air stank.

"This way," he said as he led her to the back corner, to a door that was semi-hidden behind a rack that held blankets and pillows. "My dad told me about this before he...well before he left," said Adam swallowing around the lump in his throat.

He pushed aside the blankets and pillows on the bottom shelf and squeezed to the back. The door was no larger than a child could fit through. Luckily for Adam, he and his newfound partner were both small framed. He pushed on the door but it wouldn't budge. Just then, the first piece of debris hit the earth above them. All around them, kids screamed. This was it. He had to open the door. Franticly, he pushed and pushed.

"Help me!" His companion squished in next to him and they pushed the door with all their might until, finally, it opened. They scampered inside, shut the door and leaned against it. There was little chance anyone would find the door any time soon.

"I'm Adam," he said, putting his hand out to shake hers.

Ignoring the hand and giving him a queer look she said, "My name's Eve."

DECEMBER

The snow fell from the sky. Perfect little pieces of crystal, each unique and beautiful. Cora watched from her window, longing in her heart, with every fiber of her small, fragile frame wishing she could feel them on her tongue, in her hair, on her skin but knowing that it was a wish that could never be fulfilled. For Cora, nothing could exist outside of this room. Everything outside meant death to her. Every breath, every surface, a bomb waiting to explode, taking her with it. Letting the curtain fall back into place, she wandered to her desk and switched on the monitor waiting for her.

"Good morning, Cora." said the electronic voice that greeted her at the start of each day. "Today you will be studying ancient languages..." The voice continued to drone on but Cora tuned it out as she had every day for the past month. Did it matter if she died? If, for just one time in her life, she could experience something beyond these walls? Was the life she was currently living really a life at all?

Cora doodled on the touch-pad before her, daydreams taking over her thoughts. What if she could get out? If the door of her prison ever opened and she could see a real human being, touch them, talk with them, laugh with them, wouldn't that be worth it?

"Cora!" The voice wasn't electronic. This voice was the sound she dreaded: it was her benefactor. Her warden. Her mother.

"Yes, Mother?"

"Stop daydreaming and attend to your studies this instant."

Her buttoned up form appeared in the two-way mirror that dominated the opposite side of her room. They could look in at whatever they wanted to on her side but she could only see what they chose to show her. Currently, that was her stern-looking mother in her gray buttoned-up shirt and starched floor-length skirt. Every inch of her covered except her face and hands. A face and hands that she had grown to hate. There was no love, no tenderness there. Her mother was nothing like the fairy tale mothers that she read about in the stories she secretly poured over each night after lights-out with the contraband flashlight one of the guards had snuck into the small tube that was

45

her only connection to the outside world. He had sanitized every inch of it to rid it of the germs that could kill her. The one person that showed her any compassion. Her knight in shining armor, Arnold. If her mother ever found out that Arnold had secured and supplied her with it, he would be dismissed. Cora took special care to hide the things he had given her.

"Yes, Mother." Cora sighed as she restarted the instruction she had tuned out. She knew her mother would expect a full review of the day's lessons. "But couldn't we just talk for awhile? I get so lonely." Cora had no idea why she was bothering her mother with such a request. It was so unlikely she would respond positively to it.

"Cora," her mother sighed, looking weary for the first time in her life. Cora thought she even saw sadness in her eyes. "There is nothing to talk about, and you have much to learn. I've distracted you from your studies long enough. Please, just do as you are told." With that, her mother's side of the mirror went black and Cora was left alone. Always alone.

Switching her lesson back on, "Language has been around since the dawn of time..." Cora tried to concentrate but her mind wandered elsewhere.

AUTHOR'S NOTE

I hope you've enjoyed the stories I've started for you. Use them as a jumping point off point for your own stories. You have my permission to use these beginnings as long as you tweak them to make them your own. You'll know you've reached that point when the words sound like yours and not mine. I hope that you'll be able to complete a full length novel (50,000 words or more) with one of the starters I've supplied for you. I'd love to see what you come up with! You can send me your version for critique at: bunnyminer40@gmail.com

Please note, regular critique fees apply. You can read more about my services at: bunnyminer.com.

AUTHO'S BIO

Bunny Miner is the coordinator of blogging and reviews for Xchyler Publishing. As their point of contact for bloggers and reviewers, she spends much time on the web looking for her next victims...er, um, assistants. When she's not helping the authors at Xchyler Publishing, she likes to spend her free time with her 4 crazy kids, 3 dogs, 2 rabbits (yes, she knows there's a joke in there somewhere) and 1 really cute husband. Bunny's been writing since about 2000 and has published in various trade magazines and newsletters as well as her local paper. *And So it Begins* is her first published ebook. Look for her new book, *10 Little Nephites* due out in February 2015.

If you enjoyed this group of story starters, please leave your honest review on Amazon and blog about it if you wish! Thanks for your time and investment and I look forward to reading what you've created!

Keep calm and WRITE ON!

Acknowledgements:

To my amazing family who has read, re-read and re-re-read everything I've written and not complained about it (at least to me!). To my amazing editors, Kim Bennett and MeriLyn Oblad and for Desert Shadow Publishing for taking a shot on me and my work.

www.ingramcontent.com/pod-product-compliance
Lightning Source LLC
Chambersburg PA
CBHW070624290526
45790CB00002B/984